April 2019

For Domenico + Family

The Divine Kiss

With Much
Appreciation
Love
Carolyn

The Divine Kiss

an exhibit of Paintings and Poems

in honor of David Campagna

Carolyn Mary Kleefeld

Karpeles Manuscript Library and Museum

October 3–November 30, 2013
Santa Barbara, California

May 18–June 28, 2014
Shreveport, Louisiana

The Seventh Quarry &
Cross-Cultural Communications
Wales / New York
2014

Inquiries about *The Divine Kiss* should be addressed to

Editor-Publisher: **Peter Thabit Jones**
The Seventh Quarry Press
8 Cherry Crescent
Parc Penderri
Penllerhaer, Swansea SA4 9FG Wales
info@peterthabitjones.com
www.peterthabitjones.com

Editor-Publisher: **Stanley H. Barkan**
Cross-Cultural Communications
239 Wynsum Avenue
Merrick, New York 11566-4725 USA
(516) 868-5635
(516) 379-1901 fax
cccpoetry@aol.com
www.cross-culturalcommunications.com

Carolyn Mary Kleefeld
PO Box 370
Big Sur, CA 93920
info@carolynmarykleefeld.com
www.carolynmarykleefeld.com
alchemyoracle.com

Karpeles Document Museum and Library
21 West Anapamu St.
Santa Barbara, CA 93101
(805) 962-5322

3201 Centenary Blvd.
Shreveport, LA 71104
(318) 861-7615

Inquiries about the author's artwork, fine art cards, and other books should be addressed to

Atoms Mirror Atoms, Inc.
PO Box 221693
Carmel, California 93922
(800) 403-3635
(831) 667-2226
info@carolynmarykleefeld.com
www.carolynmarykleefeld.com

Friend Carolyn Mary Kleefeld on Facebook

ISBN 978-0-89304-970-6
Library of Congress Control Number: 2014933759

Book and cover design by Li Yao
Photos of Carolyn Mary Kleefeld and David Campagna by Jai Italiander
For cover art, please see Paintings, page 45

First Printing 2014
Printed in Canada

Contents

ACKNOWLEDGMENTS

With deep gratitude to my treasured colleagues and friends:

Patricia Holt, Kirtana, Ronna Emmons, Stanley H. and Bebe Barkan, Peter Thabit Jones, Vincent Clemente, Li Yao, Laura and Frank Zabrowski, John Larson, Dennis Wyszynski, Dr. Darin Deterra, Jai Italiander, Norman Cohan, Nicholas Frangakis, Linda Jacobson, Karen and Kyla Pfeiffer, Allen Silberhartz, Sarah London, David and Marsha Karpeles, John Gillespie, Sylvia White, Cameron Hurdis, Katy Devorick, Carla Kleefeld, Celeste Worl, John Dotson, David Jay Brown, Claudia Kleefeld and Chiara de Braconier D'Alphen, Olimpia Iacob, Yoon-Ho Cho, Byoung Park, Jaihiun J. Kim, Irene S. Yoon, Kyun-Nyung Kim and Steffen Richards, Lidia Chiarelli and Gianpiero and Alessandro Actis, David Wayne Dunn, Michael Zakian, Helen Bar-Lev, Adel and Mary Gorgy, Marsha Solomon, Valerie Corral, Dr. Paul Fleiss and Jesse Fleiss, Peggy and George DiCaprio, Chungliang Al Huang, Dr. Bernfried Nugel, Edna Isman, Dr. Roberta Spurr, Barbara Simonich, Dr. Murray Susser, Ariadne Sawyer, Dr. Roy Auerbach, Natalie Van Allen, Evan Landy, Lorena Del Campo, Derek Viverretta, Stacy Valis.

Foreword

The Divine Kiss is a loving, passionate, and highly original work that inspires and evokes the lover in all of us. Here, Rumi elopes with Chagall in a dance of color, compassion, and sensuality. Carolyn Kleefeld's authentic, intelligent, and transcendent poetry takes us on a divine journey into the heart of love. Painting and poetry mirror one another, then merge together. Each poem is a multi-layered metaphor, borne of Eros, matured through Agape. The paintings dazzle, warm, and invite, making love with the prose.

Wildly enchanting, deeply moving, vulnerable yet powerful, *The Divine Kiss* caresses and transforms us. It is indeed the "kiss of a lifetime," "milk for the soul"— "sheer magic" that "silently possesses" us. This is a stunning piece of work.

Dr. Darin Deterra
therapist and author

November 2013

INTRODUCTION

Carolyn Kleefeld is a painter and poet whose work illustrates her innermost thoughts and feelings. Her romantic figuratives and poetic images embody the fabric of her life. Imbued with seemingly contrasting forces, her art expresses both opposing energies and complementary equalities: solidity and fluidity, organic masculine and feminine, yin and yang.

Beautifully rendered erotic symbolism makes her work uniquely healing. The art conveys a sense of whimsy, spontaneity, and the sheer enjoyment of shape and color. With so much light and motion, Carolyn's paintings are incredibly intriguing. The cryptic nature of the artwork entices viewers to discover their own interpretations.

The library/museum environment at the Karpeles was perfect for this select group of paintings and corresponding poems of the exhibit, *The Divine Kiss*, as it truly allowed visitors the space to fully study and contemplate each special work of art and poetry.

Painting is a kind of mute poetry and poetry a speaking picture. While painting can be appreciated for its silent being, it reaches for the addition of words, as words desire the visual sense. Gazing at the art then reading the poetry is so inspiring; I find myself transported to a completely different world.

Carolyn's "medium" is her unique visual language, visual eloquence. That is the hallmark of this amazing artist.

Jai Italiander
Ojai, California

November 2013

Selected Karpeles Reviews

To enter Carolyn Kleefeld's "aura artistica" is to recapture the rapture of creation.

To see the world through her eyes, her art, and her poetry sanctifies the marriage of Life and Love.

The moment explodes with kisses. Passionate kisses. Silent kisses. Gypsy kisses. Exotic kisses. I am spellbound by a tapestry of kisses.

Contemplating her longing for Unity, my dormant impulses are awakened.

An intense desire for Beauty and the ecstatic joy of discovery reverberate with this woman and with her art.

It is said that "she who longs the most, lives the longest."

Carolyn Kleefeld will live forever.

Norman Anu Cohan
director
Karpeles Manuscript Museum and Library

We have many people coming into our document museum specifically to see Carolyn Kleefeld's exhibit, and to enthusiastic response. It is so unusual for someone to be so poetically connected and so gifted artistically in such a prolific way. Sensual energies pervade and inspire.

Sarah London
archivist, receptionist
Karpeles Manuscript Museum and Library

That Sliver of Nothingness

*O you, who are so distant,
yet so intimate in
your silent possession of me—
Am I loving the unknown,
rather than you?*

*Is it the distance we keep
that breeds our intimacy?*

*O unknown one,
why does your voice
hold such richness—
a richness that brightens
my waning heart?*

*O breath of life,
am I searching for the stars
of a dream never to be?*

*Is there only this oblivion
outside of death?*

*Lurch me from the shadows
that leach my life.*

*Take me, embrace me
in that sliver of nothingness
that for a moment,
can feel so complete.*

Ghost Lover

Eros and Aphrodite

Hunger of the Wilds

Love me like the lightning
that strikes its beloved tree—
wild and free, with white heat
and fingers flaming.

Oh, yes, love me like the riptide
that tears across the sea
into its lover's caves.

Yes, love me like the volcano
that erupts with molten fire—
singeing the earth
with quivering caresses.

Yes, love me like
the falcons that screech and soar,
diving through heaven's blue meadows.

Oh yes, love me with
the hunger of the wilds.

I Long For You

I long for you
like twilight, the night.
Like a calf,
its mother's milk.

I long for you
like the desert, water.
Like a clock, time.

I long for you
like the moon,
the galaxies.

I long for you
like the tides, the shore.
Like flowers, water.

Although you
just left this morning—
I long for you
like the tree, its roots.
Like my breath,
air to breathe.

Erotic Rendezvous

Lovers of the Golden Fishes

Of Golden Fishes

Come to me,
O river of golden fishes.

Come to me now,
with your pagan heart
and empty hands
brimming with kisses.

Come to me now,
lover of trembling embrace
and wounded heart—
let your golden fishes
swim to the cobalt sea.

Come to me,
broken river of golden life,
and together we'll swim
to the open sea,
where our gilded fishes
and trembling kisses
gleam in the shining waters.

Come to me now,
O pagan lover
of the golden fishes;
we'll ride their
shiny, slippery backs
to the ocean of our dreams.

A Whole New Sun

His is a world
I had not entered
but now through his form,
I can.

He carries me out
of my womb caves
onto the stage of life,
offering me a whole new sun
that shines through his form.

With my hand in his,
we stroll foreign lands;
stars in our hearts,
stars in our eyes.

We speak the same silent language,
and listen to the same silent music.
Continually in re-invention,
we keep discovering one another
in the unfolding moments.

With passion as our key,
we enter one world after another,
making love in every land,
miracles manifesting our way of life.

Feral Passion

Psyche and Eros

Borne of Eros

Our fountain,
borne of Eros,
cascades into poems—
lyrics of love
you murmur to my soul.

These rhapsodies flower
my inner gardens.
I'm all abloom with you.
Enraptured.

We are each other's
muse and mirror, merging
in a blaze of passion—
our currents, incandescent.

And the phoenix of our love
rises beyond all thorns
birthing unforeseen dawns.

Lovers of Lake Como

We sip from
this lake azure
filled with the treasures
of an ancient allure.

Spellbound; we glide
into the present,
and joyfully partake,
imbibing the paradise
of this legendary lake.

Ancient marble terraces
and crystal chandeliers
glitter as we stroll.
Captivating melodies
and gold baroque mirrors
echo reflections of our souls.

Roman deities,
eternal muses and sages
still reside here,
embroidering us
into the tapestry of the ages.

Lovers at Lake Como

Divine Kiss

The Kiss

Tonight, the kiss I've dreamed of,
the kiss of a lifetime, is here.

And now we hug and kiss
and kiss and love—
exploding the moment,
as if we were an extravagant bouquet
of burgeoning flowers and stamens.

Like creatures dashing through the forest,
we tumble into each other's arms,
our mouths and leafy boughs entwined.

Some strange and wondrous magnet
is drawing us together
like orbiting stars, carrying us
beyond the dust of ourselves.

A Resonance of Glory

I'm possessed, haunted
by the memory of our magic,
our adventure into
the realm of the Beloved.

My flesh still tingles
at the thought of your caress.

O darling one,
you birth Eros
in my heart
as garlands of wildflowers
petal our path.

You bring to earth
a resonance of glory—
the ancient lyrics of eternal love.

Mirrored Souls

Carnal Love

Milk for the Soul

She waited for him,
like a lactating mother,
all full of her own flesh
as if she were going to feed him
when he arrived.
But from the Unseen,
the milk would come.

Below her tower,
cream rose from the sea.
And the starry night's nipples,
offered their gleam
from galactic orchards.

Yes, there would be a cornucopia
awaiting her beloved knight
when he arrived tonight
on the mountaintop.

There she would be wearing,
close to her skin,
a raiment of love
spun from her body and soul,
the flesh of the sun,
and the gold of
surrounding meadows.

Her heart robed in moonlight
would offer him a silvery embrace,
and the milk of her soul
would feed him forever.

Have Mercy, Eros

Captivated by your spell,
the potion of your passion,
the mystery of our fusion,
I am humbled,
bound in prayer
to the greater love
that feeds us
such unfurling magic.

Yet, I wander this night
of mercurial moon, singing
from haunted chambers
of my longing for you.

The void seems to mock me,
for I have become
a wild creature
gripped by the leash
of a feverish passion,
eagerly awaiting
our next encounter.

Have mercy, Eros!

A Cartoon Mocking Life

Guardian

In Gratitude

Hungry with longing,
I wait for you.

When you call,
I am filled
with the wine
that needs no cup.

Thank you for
letting me long for you,
for giving me
the time and space
to wander in the unknown,
the mystical meadows
of the limitless void.

How else could I
have discovered
the elusive magic
found in the silent hours?

And aren't
the nights of longing
a prelude to the gold
of our consummation?

Sheer Magic

Aroused by
your tender embrace,
I bloom like sheer magic
orchestrated by the divine.

Like quintessential chords,
we merge, dancing
in the shifting light,
wondrous to behold.

Our sublime moments unfurl
in an exotic twirl,
as we emit the musk of all lovers
lost beyond time.

Zen Lovers

Enigmatic Love

Wild Gypsies Play

While animals rove
and voices erupt
from the pitched tents
at the Arab Camp
we play like wild gypsies next door.

As another kind of creature,
you come as if by magic,
lapping me up in loving arms.

Our passion lights a fire
flowering this desert
as we join the savannahs
of twinkling stars.

Here at our gypsy caravan,
wrapped within each other's arms,
we transcend even ourselves.

A Magical Synchronicity

Intuitively, I explore
the invisible realms
and find you
bravely striding
through the jungle
of concrete and man.

As if hearing a bell,
I know just when to call.
And the magic of
our synchronicity chimes on
with a life of its own
that we tune into
as if we were notes
in a rhapsodic chord,
humming in vibration
with the eternal symphony.

Blesséd Lovers

In honor of

We make fantasy into reality . . .

David Campagna

From the Artist

. . . and, my artwork records our dance.

Carolyn Mary Kleefeld

About the Author

Born in Catford, England, Carolyn grew up in southern California, where she studied art and psychology at UCLA. In 1980 she moved to her cliff-side home high above the Pacific Ocean in Big Sur, where she studies, writes, and paints amidst the surrounding wilderness.

A passion for creative expression and a lifelong fascination with spiritual transformation have propelled Carolyn to become an award-winning poet, writer, and artist. She is the author of twelve books, a variety of which are used as inspirational texts in universities and healing centers, and are featured along with the writings of seven other acclaimed woman writers in a continuing course, "The Other Half of the Sky: Eight Woman Writers," at Swansea University in Wales. Carolyn's poems have been nominated for the Pushcart Prize. Her first book, *Climates of the Mind,* was translated into Braille by the Library of Congress. Her writings have been translated into Korean, Romanian, Arabic, and Bulgarian. *Vagabond Dawns* and *Soul Seeds: Revelations and Drawings* are published in bilingual English-Korean editions, and *Vagabond Dawns* is published in a bilingual English-Romanian edition, with a bilingual English-Romanian edition of *Soul Seeds* forthcoming in the summer of 2014.

Over the past three decades, Carolyn has created an extensive and diverse body of paintings and drawings, ranging in style from romantic figurative to abstract. The Frederick R. Weisman Museum of Art at Pepperdine University exhibited a retrospective of Carolyn's paintings and drawings in 2008 and published a catalog, *Carolyn Mary Kleefeld: Visions from Big Sur,* with commentary by Michael Zakian, PhD, curator and director. Carolyn's art is featured internationally in galleries, museums, private collections, and multimedia presentations.

PO Box 370
Big Sur, California 93920
(800) 403-3635
(831) 667-2226
info@carolynmarykleefeld.com
www.carolynmarykleefeld.com
alchemyoracle.com

Friend Carolyn Mary Kleefeld on Facebook

Carolyn Mary Kleefeld Publications

Psyche of Mirrors: A Promenade of Portraits (prose, poems, and art)
Preface by Peter Thabit Jones, Introduction by Vince Clemente, Foreword by Deanna McKinstry-Edwards
The Seventh Quarry/Cross-Cultural Communications, Swansea, Wales, and Merrick, NY 2012

Poet to Poet #4: Poems—East Coast/West Coast (poems)
With Stanley H. Barkan
The Seventh Quarry/Cross-Cultural Communications, Swansea, Wales, and Merrick, NY 2010

Vagabond Dawns (poems, with CD)
Foreword by David Wayne Dunn, Prologue by Professor-Doctor Bernfried Nugel
Cross-Cultural Communications, Merrick, NY 2009

Soul Seeds: Revelations and Drawings (philosophical aphorisms and art)
Foreword by Laura Archera Huxley
Cross-Cultural Communications, Merrick, NY 2008

Carolyn Mary Kleefeld: Visions from Big Sur (catalog from exhibit, Frederick R. Weisman Museum of Art)
Art with commentary by Michael Zakian, PhD
Pepperdine University, Malibu, CA 2008

Kissing Darkness: Love Poems and Art (poems and art)
Co-authored with David Wayne Dunn
RiverWood Books, Ashland, OR 2003

The Alchemy of Possibility: Reinventing Your Personal Mythology
(prose, poetry, and art, with quotes from the Tarot and *I Ching;* can serve as an oracle)
Foreword by Laura Archera Huxley
Merrill-West Publishing, Carmel, CA 1998; 2nd edition 2013
See *alchemyoracle.com*

Mavericks of the Mind: Conversations for the New Millennium
(interviews with Allen Ginsberg, Terence McKenna, Timothy Leary, Laura Archera Huxley, Carolyn Mary Kleefeld, *et al.*)
By David Jay Brown and Rebecca Novick
The Crossing Press, Freedom, CA 1993; 2nd edition by Maps, Santa Cruz, CA 2010

Songs of Ecstasy, Limited Edition (poems)
Atoms Mirror Atoms, Carmel, CA 1990

Songs of Ecstasy
(art booklet with poems commemorating Carolyn's solo exhibition and poetry reading at Gallerie Illuminati, Santa Monica, CA)
Atoms Mirror Atoms, Carmel, CA 1990

Lovers in Evolution (poems and photographs from Mt. Palomar Observatory)
The Horse and Bird Press, Los Angeles, CA 1983

Satan Sleeps with the Holy: Word Paintings (poems)
The Horse and Bird Press, Los Angeles, CA 1982

Climates of the Mind (poems and philosophical aphorisms)
The Horse and Bird Press, Los Angeles, CA 1979 (4th printing)

About My Art

Art, like music, offers a language beyond words. To be innovative, it must be created from an inner wilderness, free of stale and redundant concepts.

If art arises from an inner necessity to express rather than from a preconceived idea of beauty or style, then it can reflect, in symbolic imagery, our primal nature and oneness with all things.

Through the instrument of my being, I let my intuition choose color and form, an experiment comparable to musical improvisation.

For me art is a spontaneous journey on the crest of the Tao's wave, an exploration born of passion, spawned by the Mystery. Initially, I am the maiden falling in love—then later, the ruthless editor-analyst.

Ultimately art is an innocent interactive mirror of my innermost process, whisking me out of time into the Timeless. My life's passion is to create art from this unconditioned well of being and to inspire such a journey in others.

Carolyn Mary Kleefeld

Paintings

Page 11
Ghost Lover (2008)
Oil on canvas, 30 x 32 in.

Page 12
Eros and Aphrodite (2009)
Oil on canvas, 36 x 48 in.

Page 15
Erotic Rendezvous (2009)
Oil on canvas, 48 x 36 in.

Page 16
Lovers of the Golden Fishes (2010)
Acrylic on canvas, 48 x 36 in.

Page 19
Feral Passion (2012)
Oil on canvas, 24 x 18 in.

Page 20
Psyche and Eros (2012)
Oil and Arylic on canvas, 36 x 30 in.

Page 23
Lovers at Lake Como (2012)
Mixed media on canvas, 24 x 24 in.

Page 24
Divine Kiss (2012)
Oil on canvas, 20 x 20 in.

Page 27
Mirrored Souls (2013)
Oil on canvas, 36 x 30 in.

Page 28
Carnal Love (2013)
Oil on canvas, 20 x 16 in.

Page 31
A Cartoon Mocking Life (2013)
Acrylic on canvas, 36 x 30 in.

Page 32
Guardian (2013)
Arylic on canvas, 24 x 24 in.

Page 35
Zen Lovers (2013)
Oil and Acrylic on canvas, 24 x 24 in.

Page 36
Enigmatic Love (2013)
Acrylic on canvas, 24 x 18 in.

Page 39
Blesséd Lovers (2013)
Acrylic on canvas, 48 x 36 in.

Notes

Notes

And the phoenix of our love
rises beyond all thorns
birthing unforeseen dawns.